The Basics of Life Insurance

The Answers to What Life Insurance is and How it Works

By Kirk G. Meyer

Basics of Life Insurance: The Answers to
What Life Insurance is and How it Works

Copyright © 2014 by Kirk G. Meyer

Table of Contents

Introduction

There are two main types of life insurance and then several variations of each type. Life insurance can be classified as term and permanent. At least that is the simplified explanation of the two types of life insurance. The most common life insurance policies can be placed into the following categories: term, whole life, universal life, variable life, and variable universal life. Each one of these insurances has a place in one's life and at different times in someone's life they may have need of one or a combination of these types of insurance products. Depending on your circumstances, you may or may not even have a need for life insurance. Everyone's situation is different and therefor the need of life insurance will vary dramatically from individual to individual and from family to family. In order for life insurance to be effective and useful there are many things that need to be considered when buying a policy. In the following pages we will examine the difference between term and permanent life insurance, the differences between the various types of permanent insurance, and what products are right for those seeking life insurance.

Types of Life Insurance

First let's examine the most common type of life insurance and that is term insurance. As the name implies the insurance is in place for a period of normally 5, 10, 15, 20, or 30 years. This insurance is normally the least expensive as it provides a death benefit only and does not accumulate any cash value. The policy will help provide security for the named beneficiary in the event the insured dies and the coverage is only for the length of the term. If the insured does not die during the term no benefits will be observed and the cost of the policy will be the premiums paid to the insurance company. A term policy is mainly used when coverage is needed only for a certain period of time or if the insured has limited funds available for life insurance. As the policy does not accumulate any assets and is for a limited period of time the premiums will be lower than that of a permanent insurance product. By design the lower the premiums paid will allow for the insured to obtain a higher face value for their death benefit. As the insurer gets older and chooses to renew their policy the premiums will be higher which is a negative of term insurance. But if the insured is younger term insurance can provide a large amount of death benefits at a very reasonable premium cost.

Some term policies are renewed on an annual basis with the premiums increasing every year while others renew on the anniversary of the expiration of the term. Also, most term policy have the ability to be converted to permanent policies at the option of the insured for a fee. Both of these options can be done with no need to provide proof of insurability due to the fact you already are insured with the company, thereby you will not need additional underwriting. This is an advantage of getting a term policy when you are younger and in theory healthier than when you are older and may find yourself difficult to insure due to health concerns. In that instance you are not only providing security for the insured's family, they are enabling themselves to convert a term policy to a permanent one when they otherwise might not be able to obtain the insurance.

The premiums paid for term insurance are considered level as they do not change as long as the policy is in effect. If the policy is a 30 year term policy the premiums will be consistent for the entire 30 year period. An annual term is guaranteed for one year but is not really a level term policy its year by year nature and the fact the premiums will increase every year it renews. Any time a policy is renewed the insurance company will adjust the premiums to a higher amount due to the increased likelihood the insured could die during the policy. That is one reason term insurance is so reasonable for younger people and is good for families starting out is the likelihood that they will die during the term is lower than an older person's likelihood of dying. Premiums for term insurance are also higher the longer the term is, again due to the likelihood that the insured could die during the term's period.

Generally a 10 year term policy's premium would be less expensive than a 30 year term policy for the same individual.

There is also a second type of term policy and that is one that is a decreasing term policy. These policies generally have a level premium but the death benefit will decrease over time. They are generally used as mortgage protection products for people seeking to protect their primary residence in the event they were to die prior to their mortgage being paid off.

The next four insurance types will be permanent insurance products as compared to the term product. The main differences between permanent and term insurance is permanent insurance generally have a higher premium, may have a constant level premium over the life of the policy, build cash value, and covers the life of the insured. Now let's look at the main four types of permanent life insurance.

Whole life insurance provides the insured with a guaranteed insurance protection for the life of the insured or until they cease making the premium payments. Unlike term insurance whole life has a cash value component to it that actually makes owning the life insurance policy an asset. A portion of the premium goes to pay for the life insurance and a portion goes to making up the cash value which has a guaranteed a minimum rate of return that grows tax deferred. Like term insurance the premium is level for the life of the policy and the death benefit is a known constant.

As for how the premium of whole life works it is a multi-part premium. First part of the premium goes to pay for the life insurance itself, second there are administrative fees that the insurance company charges, and the final part goes to the investment component of the policy or the cash value. And gains in the cash value are tax deferred and taxes are based on your cost basis at the time the funds are withdrawn. An example is your cash value is

$100,000 and your cost basis was $80,000 you are only liable for taxes on the $20,000 difference between the two values. The basis is calculated by premiums paid by you minus dividends if any were paid and any previous withdrawals. The amount of a withdrawal that is over your basis is taxed as ordinary income and not at a capital gains rate. As this policy is permanent the premium is higher and after the insured has accumulated a substantial cash value they can actually use that pool of money to pay your premiums until such time that the value is decreased to zero. This type of policy is both an insurance policy and a savings account in a manner of speaking.

Universal life is another type of permanent life insurance that is similar to whole life in certain respects but it is considered flexible or adjustable life. Like whole life it is a permanent policy that accumulates a cash value component based on current interest rates. Unlike whole life universal life allows the insured to adjust the death benefit as their needs change. The premiums are also adjustable depending on the level of the death benefit that the insured desires resulting in higher premiums for a higher death benefit and a lower premium for a lower death benefit. Also, as the premiums are adjustable to match the death benefit and the value that is accumulated in the cash value portion is also a variable. That does not mean someone who purchases a universal life product has to adjust their death benefits or premiums but it is an option to whole life where both are set at the beginning of the policy.

Variable life is the third type of permanent life insurance which relies on two components making up the policy and is similar to whole life. One is the life insurance benefit and the other is a savings feature that is allowed to grow in certain investment vehicles. On one side is the general account which consists of the portion of the premiums that go towards paying for the life insurance death benefit and is not allocated to any one policy that the company issues. The other component has various investment funds that are within the insurance company's investment profile which could be equities, money markets, bonds, or any combination. Due to the investment portion of the product, the cash value and death benefit have the possibility of fluctuating hence the name variable life. This life insurance product is different from whole life and universal life and is classified as a security and therefor has to be sold by a licensed life insurance agent as well as a licensed securities dealer.

The fourth and final permanent life insurance product is variable universal life. This product allows the insured to adjust the premiums, death benefits, and still have the flexibility of investing excess funds for growth. Like the variable type of permanent policies this one is also classified as an investment and thereby needs to be sold not only by a licensed life insurance agent but also a licensed securities dealer. That means variable and variable universal policies are regulated by both the state in which they are issued and the Securities and Exchange Commission. In these policies all of the risk of the policy is with the insured and not the insurance company. That means that the death benefit may go up or down depending on how successful the investments made by the insured does. But many insurance companies that issue this type of policy may also issue some kind of guarantee that at least a minimum death benefit will be paid to the policy's beneficiary with the exception of variable universal life.

Many people who want permanent life insurance but need a higher death benefit for a certain period of time. While a universal life policy allows for the insured to change the death benefit it may not be the most practical or economical chose of products. As an alternative the insured can buy a whole life policy for the amount they believe will be needed in their older age and buy a term policy at the same time to cover the need for a higher death benefit for that period of time. This approach is normally cheaper and makes more sense than buying the higher priced universal life policy by itself.

Differences in Permanent Insurance, Whole and Universal

As we looked at briefly in the previous section there are several types of permanent life insurance but two in general are whole life and universal life. The other two will not be discussed here because they resemble more of a security than an insurance product. While both whole and universal are permanent insurance products there are indeed some differences that you need to be aware of prior to purchasing either one. As we will discuss later, the methods that one might consider before buying life insurance include the needs of one's loved ones before and after their death. Whole life is geared towards long-term goals by offering the insured a fixed death benefit, constant premiums, and a guaranteed cash value. Universal life is also geared towards long-term needs but provides the insurer flexibility in premiums and the death benefit while also providing a cash value savings element as well. While the differences are subtle whole life as a rule has a higher premium than universal as with anything that is financial in nature you will pay a premium for the guaranteed components of the policy.

While both permanent and term insurance provide the insured and their loved ones financial security when the insured dies permanent insurance may be consider more desirable over term for long-term planning. This is one of the reasons why many insurance companies will allow a term policy to be converted to a permanent policy with no additional underwriting by using a rider for this protection. In these instances the insured will gain the benefit of a permanent policy despite any new health concerns with an increase in the premiums that will be paid to the insurance company. The key to remember between term life and permanent life is term life is considered a temporary insurance that will only last for a predetermined period of time while a permanent policy will be for the rest of the insured's life or until they decide to stop paying premiums and withdrawal the cash value of the policy.

Permanent life insurance policies are two fold as stated before, there is a life insurance component and a savings component. Term policies on the other hand simply have a life insurance component that the premium pays for. For this reason premiums for permanent insurance have a much higher premiums and whole life will have a higher premium then universal life, again due to the guaranteed portion of the policy. As such the excess funds paid in premiums are invested by the insurance company and any interest the investments make grow tax deferred making up the cash value of the policy. One of the features of a permanent policy is that the insured can actually take a loan out against the accumulated cash value of the policy. Please note that there are two values at work in a permanent policy and that is the built up cash value and the face value or death benefit the insured's beneficiaries will see upon their death. It is important to remember that when the insured borrow against their cash value they borrow against that amount and not the amount of the death benefit. Loans against the cash value of a permanent life insurance policy do have the benefit of having low interest rates, the proceeds may be used in any legal manner the insured desires, and there are no credit issues as the loan is not reported to any credit agencies.

Another benefit of having a permanent life insurance policy is that it has accumulated a cash value that the insured may use to pay the premiums in the event they are experiencing a financial hardship. But in the event the insured does not pay their premium and there is insufficient value in the cash value portion their policy may be terminated or it could be converted into a reduced paid-up policy. Many people who have permanent policies let the cash value save up to the point where when they retire they have enough accumulated in the policy to pay the premiums in their retirement years. The problem with this approach is the insured may outlive the number of premiums that can be paid out of the cash value resulting in their need to restart paying the premiums or risk having the policy canceled.

In the event the insured wishes to cancel their permanent policy they will receive the value accumulated in the cash value portion of the policy. There may be tax consequences to taking the cash value out of an insurance policy so consider consulting a tax advisor to ensure you are compliant with all tax laws. Also, as permanent insurance is meant to be for the lifetime of the insured it is costly to take a policy out and then cancel it so consider term insurance in the event you will only need to have insurance for a period of time and not your entire lifetime.

Now whole life will provide the insured with insurance for their entire life or as long as they make the premium payments. This type of policy provides a level premium and a constant face death benefit. As a general rule this type of policy is kept in force for the rest of the insured's life no matter how long they live. Again, this type of permanent coverage provides a life insurance and savings component to the premiums. In a whole life policy the value of the cash value portion is guaranteed making it costly as compared to a term policy, especially early on in the policy's life cysle. These premiums look more attractive as the insured ages and may be even considered cheap if the policy was taken out when they were very young. A whole life policy will be more expensive for an older individual as the insurance company has a shorter period of time to collect enough premiums to cover the death benefit. A younger individual thereby has a longer period of time to fund the death benefit resulting in more premiums but at a lower cost.

In a whole life policy the insurance company places a portion of the premium in what is essentially a high-yield bank account. And as a portion of every premium goes to fund the savings side of the policy, every premium payment will increase your cash value. Again the cash value of a life insurance policy grows tax deferred making it advantageous to a bank savings account that will be taxed. Again the insured can borrow against the cash value, use it to pay the policy's premiums, or cancel the policy and take the accumulated cash. A feature that provides an additional source of funds in these policies is an insurance company may have a surplus of cash and opt to pay dividends to policy owners. This is more common in fraternal insurance companies as they do not have shareholders who expect any profits to be passed to them and not the policy holders. Now the insured may obtain and use the dividends in a few different ways. The more common options are to take the dividends in cash, let them be placed in the cash value to accumulate more interest, reduce your policy premiums, or buy additional coverage. If you are not certain as to what is best you may consider consulting a financial planner or an insurance advisor.

The other common type of permanent insurance is universal life sometimes referred to as adjustable life insurance. Compared to whole life, universal life is more flexible and can be changed as the insured's needs change. As an example of an insured's needs changing someone who is young may need enough coverage to provide their loved ones with loss of income, educational expenses, or to pay off a mortgage. This same person later in life may only need to supply their loved ones with a loss of income as the mortgage may be paid off and their children are out of school. In this respect universal life is very convenient for someone who needs to plan long-term but may not need the same level of death benefit throughout their life. In the event the insured wishes to increase their death benefit they will need to pass a medical examination. Conversely the insured may be charged a surrender fee when they reduce a death benefit that could be charged against their cash value. Also once the first premium is paid to the insurance company the insured has some flexibility to reduce or increase their premium and possibly pay them at any time provided they fall within the policies of the insurance company that issued the policy.

The death benefit of a universal life policy has two options for payment. One is a fixed death benefit that will be paid to the beneficiary and the second is an increasing death benefit equal to the face value of the death benefit plus the cash value that has been accumulated. Unlike a whole policy a universal policy allows the insured to change the amount and frequency of their premium payments. Some policies even will provide for a lump sum payment provided it is with the policy guidelines. The cash value of a universal policy grows in the same manner as a while life policy in that excess premiums are invested and grow tax deferred. Also like a whole life policy the cash value may be used to pay premiums, have loans taken out against it, or collected by the insured in the event the policy is canceled. Universal life policies will also have a disclosure of what the cost of the insurance is so the insured has a good understanding of how the policy works. One negative concerning a universal policy is that the interest rate is not guaranteed like it is in a whole life policy. When the investment is doing well the cash value accumulates faster and when the investments are not doing as well the premiums could be higher in order to accumulate the cash value.

More Permanent Insurance, Variable and Variable Universal

If you are looking for permanent life you do have options beyond whole and universal life products. In addition to those two type of permanent policies you can also choose from variable and variable universal life products. The main difference between whole and universal and these two options is that as the insured you are able to take advantage of the gains in equity markets or another market and not just an interest return mainly associated with whole and universal life products. There are some differences between variable and variable universal life and each product will be detailed in this section.

Unlike whole life or universal life where a small portion of your premium is invested in safer investments that result in gains slightly better than those offered by a bank certificate of deposit. In a variable policy the majority of your premium is invested in one or more of the insurance company's investment accounts. In a variable life product the insured has the ability to invest in such things as fixed-income funds, individual equities, mutual funds, bonds, money market accounts, or other such investments that the insurance company offers. Any profits that are made from the investments are used to increase the cash value of the policy. Similarly if the investments lose money the cash value of the policy will decrease. As with any investment there is risk and depending on the insured's risk tolerance will dictate which type of investments should be made within the variable life insurance policy. Also as the insured's risk tolerance changes they have the ability to change the investments within their policy provided it falls within the insurance company's policies. Most insurance companies have professional money managers who will invest the insured's funds after they decide on what asset classes they would like to have their premiums invested. This way the insured has the benefit of professional money management and they do not have to try and determine what investments will be the best for them to invest. By having a professional manager invest the funds, risk can be managed to a degree but not eliminated.

Now as you can see, there is an added risk reward relationship with a variable life product compared to the safer whole life or universal life products. In a variable policy the cash value depends on how well the investments do and the death benefit may also change depending on the return on the investments. This means if your investments do well the insured's cash value and death benefit will increase but the reverse is also true, if the investment decline in value the cash value and death benefit will decline. Most variable policies will offer a guaranteed minimum death benefit regardless of how the investments do in the portfolio. In order to have a guaranteed minimum death benefit the insured will have to make additional premiums as an insurance company will not risk losing its money due to poor performance of the investments. While a guaranteed death benefit is available there is no such guarantee on the insured's cash value component of the policy. Just like other permanent policies a loan may be taken against the accumulated cash value provided the amount is substantial and the risk level of the investments is acceptable. A variable policies cash value account enjoys the same tax deferred status as a whole life or universal policy.

Unlike whole and universal life products the variable product is considered a security and as a result can only be sold be a life insurance agent who also is a securities dealer. These policies will have a life insurance component and the investment side will be accompanied by a prospectus on the type of investment the insured decides on. It is important that the insured read and understand the investment's prospectus so they will understand the associated risks with that particular investment.

The final type of permanent life insurance is a variable universal life. As the name implies it is a variable policy that also has a universal life component. This makes this policy chose a popular one as it allows the insured to invest how they see fit as well as having the ability to vary their life insurance component. As with a universal policy a variable universal policy allows the insured to determine the amount and frequency of the premium payments within limits. This policy also has a feature that allows for certain lump sum premium payments as well depending on the guidelines of the policy and insurance company.

Just as in a universal policy proof of adequate health may be required if the insured decides to increase their death benefit and surrender charges may be charged in the event the death benefit is decreased. The death benefit in a variable universal life policy can be either fixed or variable equal to the cash value portion of the account. Both the cash value and the death benefit will vary according to the investments as a whole. As the entire value of the policy can decrease a variable universal life policy generally does not offer a minimum guaranteed death benefit.

A variable universal policy also enjoys the benefit of profits growing in a tax deferred account. Loans are also allowed in a variable universal policy provided they meet the same requirements of the variable policy. Depending on how the insured's investments preform, a poor performance could result in an increase in the premiums that need to be paid in order to maintain the policy. And just as a variable policy a variable universal life policy can only be sold by a licensed life insurance agent and who is also registered securities dealer.

You and Your Policy

As things go in one's life, there may be no more important choice than purchasing the right life insurance and in the correct amount to protect your loved ones. If someone is single and do not have much debt there may not be much of a need for them to have a large life insurance policy. If your family has a history of medical issues it may indeed make sense to take out a term policy with the intention of converting it at a later date as no additional underwriting will be required if you are concerned about the cost of the premiums. Also whole life, while more expensive when you are younger, can be a good value over the long run as it provides a constant death benefit at a level premium. If you think you may develop any medical conditions these are your two best options as a variable life policy will require a medical examination if you increase the face value of the death benefit. A well thought out life insurance policy can provide the insured peace of mind if they have a young family, provide low interest loans if the policy is a permanent life policy, establish wealth for your beneficiaries, and in the end provide a death benefit as well.

Besides buying the right policy it is very important to name a proper beneficiary and to keep it up to date. Too often people get a divorce, the beneficiary dies before the insured, or the insured simply changes their mind as to who they want to be named. If you do not name a beneficiary the proceeds at your time of death with be included in the insured's estate and then disbursed according to your will or at the discretion of a probate judge in the event you die intestate. Also by naming a beneficiary the death benefit will pass to them income tax free. Naming a beneficiary will also make the transfer of your death benefit easier than it would be otherwise. As the insured you may have one or more beneficiaries listed on the policy. In the event the beneficiary is a minor there are certain steps that can be taken to ensure they benefit from the policy's proceeds. In many instances trusts are established with the death benefit for minors, special needs individuals, and in some instances grown members of the insured's family. Some insurance companies that are fraternal may have restrictions that the named beneficiary must be a family members of the insured's.

Beneficiary designations can be revocable or irrevocable in nature. A revocable beneficiary can be changed by the insured to name a different individual or individuals. Normally this may be done at any point during the life of the policy owner. Technically as the insured may name their estate as the beneficiary creditors may be able to go after the proceeds of the death benefit if they do go to your estate. An irrevocable beneficiary is one that cannot be changed without an agreement between the insured and the one named as the beneficiary. As it takes the consent of the beneficiary to name a new one these funds will not be considered an asset of the insured's unless they name their estate as the beneficiary. Regardless of who the beneficiary is the proceeds may be income tax free to the beneficiary but they will be considered part of the insured's taxable estate unless the policy is placed and owned in an Irrevocable Life Insurance Trust. This is a trust established to give the insured gifting ability while they are alive up to the maximum gift allowed by tax law and provided the beneficiary is given the choice between taking the cash or having the trust pay the life insurance premium for another year. As the trust owns the policy and beneficiaries have been named the proceeds of the death benefit will pass to them income tax free and it will not be counted in the insured's taxable estate. But you really need to be sure as to the beneficiary as these are irrevocable and to change the beneficiary will normally involve a judge.

If the insured does not have a sufficient cash value accumulated to pay their premiums or they are in a financial position that does not allow them to pay their premiums their policy will lapse. In these instances for whatever reason the insured missed their premium payment thereby giving the insurance company the option to cancel their policy or reduce the coverage to a point equivalent to the total premiums paid also known as a paid-up policy. In many instances the issuing insurance company will allow the insured to renew the policy but this will vary from insurance company to insurance company.

If you are the owner of a permanent life insurance policy it will accumulate a cash value. Provided there is a substantial amount accumulated in the cash value it is possible to surrender or cancel the policy and receive the cash that has been accumulating tax deferred. In the event the cash value is higher than the cost basis the insured will owe income tax on the difference. In order to have a cash value a portion of the premium paid is used to fund the savings portion of the life insurance policy. In the event you have a substantial cash value there are several options that may be available to you. One option is the insured may cancel the policy and get the cash value paid to them directly. A second option is to have the cash value exchanged for a reduced coverage for the remaining term of the policy with no future premiums. A third option is for the policy with term insurance using the cash value to pay the premiums. And a fourth option is to have the cash value used to pay the future premiums of the permanent life insurance policy. These four options are fairly standard but could differ slightly from company to company. As permanent life insurance was purchased for the long-term none of these steps should be taken without first considering all of the options available at the time. For best results and for the best use of the cash value consult a financial planner or an insurance advisor.

As stated previously, if you have a permanent life policy that has a substantial cash value accumulated it is possible to take a loan out against that value. Many people will do this in the event of a liquidity issue or an emergency that is unforeseen. Now these loans must be repaid to the insurance company of they could be deducted from the face value of the death benefit. A loan from your life insurance company also has low interest rates as you are technically borrowing your own money and part of the proceeds may be taxable in the event you die prior to paying the loan back. Also if you are not able to pay the loan back the life insurance company may use your cash value in order to settle the loan in full.

Life Insurance May Provide Peace of Mind

You are not alone if you are wondering if you need to have life insurance. Chances are if you are single and do not have much in the way of debt you do not need that much in the way of life insurance. In this case you really only need enough to cover what little debt you have and to cover your final expenses such as your funeral and to settle your estate. However, if you are married or have a young family your insurance needs will be vastly different than that of a single individual. Chances are that if someone depends on you financially you have a need for life insurance in some form or another. And if that is the case it is better to start looking for your insurance now and not place your loved ones in a bad position in the event you die early in life. By having a solid life insurance policy in place you ensure your loved ones will be financially secure when you are no longer there to provide for them.

After you determine that you do indeed need life insurance you will have to decide if you will purchase a term or permanent policy.

So now that you have decided you need life insurance it is wise to insure anyone in the family who contributes to the financial wellbeing of that family with life insurance. That means if both parents work, both should have some form of life insurance in place at least while there are dependents who rely on the family for assistance. That normally means until the youngest child is finished with their college education. But this is not a hard rule to follow in today's society when it is common for grandparents to assist with the raising of their grandchildren while helping to support an adult child who is in need. Also if you have a heavy burden of debt it is a good idea to also maintain a sufficient level of life insurance to cover your debts, be that consumer loans, credit cards, or a mortgage. In the event you have a large estate that will be left to your loved ones many financial planners will suggest using a life insurance policy naming the estate as the beneficiary in order to pay estate taxes as death benefits are income tax free but will be considered part of the taxable estate. By having the proceeds of the life insurance policy left to your estate the death benefit can be used to pay the estate taxes in place of having to sell assets that may or may not be liquid in nature.

In order to qualify for most life insurance the person being insured will normally have to undergo a medical exam of some sort. Many life insurance companies will offered simplified policies to people provided they have clean medical histories and the death benefit is not usually over $250,000. Insurance companies will also consider your lifestyle such as drinking and smoking, any dangerous employments or hobbies, and driving record to name just a few. Three factors that influence the insured's premium without anything else being considered is age, gender, and if you smoke or not. Regardless of any other factor these three issues have a very direct impact on the premium you will pay for your life insurance.

The following are some things to consider when purchasing any type of life insurance coverage. Certain amounts are cheaper to insure and are considered a break point level such as $100,000, $250,000, and $500,000 and so forth. Always obtain an illustration for any policy you chose and if the company will not provide you with one it is best to go with a different carrier that will provide an illustration. When it is time to purchase try to always go with a level premium policy as it is preferred and you can avoid any surprises in the future concerning your premium payment. Never buy permanent insurance for the savings component as you can buy level term and invest the difference in a low priced mutual fund or a low priced exchange traded fund and get a better return over the long run. Buy the insurance that fits your need and not what an aggressive insurance agent is selling. In other words there is no need to buy a permanent policy when you only need a 15 year term policy. Always check the financial stability of any insurance company you are considering buying a policy from as you will need them to be in business not only in the near term but possibly for many decades.

How Much Insurance Do You Need

There are two primary methods to figure out how much life insurance you may need. The first method is human-life approach where the insured project the value of the insured's life for their remaining expectancy and find the present value of the need using a discount rate. The second is the needs approach which is an estimate of all reoccurring and unexpected expenditures that will occur and determine the amount of insurance that will be needed. One method is not better than the other and in many instances someone may use a combination of the two methods to come up with an amount that they are comfortable buying.

First off remember not everyone is in need of life insurance so each situation is unique to that individual or family. Look at your situation and first determine if you do in fact need a life insurance policy as there is no need to pay for something you do not really need. But as it was stated earlier it is sometimes better to purchase the insurance while you qualify for it and then not be able to qualify for it when you do in fact have a need for it later in life. And if you have any dependents or anyone for that matter who depends on your financially it makes sense and is prudent for you to have some level of life insurance to protect those loved ones who do depend on you.

A misnomer that is perpetuated by aggressive insurance agents is it is harder to qualify for insurance if you are older. Yes older people may have more health issues but provided you are relatively healthy you will qualify for insurance regardless of your age. That is why it is suggested you may want to obtain your insurance when you are younger if you have a family history of certain medical illnesses otherwise you will find an insurance company that will insure you it will just charge you a higher premium. Otherwise people have to pass the same medical examination, not have a history of certain illnesses, and be relatively healthy no matter their age. Now the younger you are when you obtain the insurance the lower your premium will be because the insurance company is making an assumption that you will live many more years until they will have to pay out the death benefit. While you may enjoy a lower premium you will in theory be paying it out longer over a longer period of time. An older person who gets the same coverage has a much shorter period of time in which to pay the insurance company its premiums. Regardless of your age insurance companies are taking the risk as to when you will die and they are in business to make money so they will rely on you paying enough premiums to cover the face value of the death benefit. If the insured has term insurance and does not die during the term the insurance company has made a profit. But on the other hand if someone purchased a 30 year term policy and died three years into the policy the insurance company has lost money. Insurance companies use sophisticated formulas to determine how much someone's premium is and they estimate how long the insured will be making premium payments.

Again never buy a life insurance policy as an investment as when looked at in that light they are poor investment choices as the returns are relatively low compared to other financial tools at your disposal and is considered expensive compared to other true investments. It is very important to buy a policy that fits your need and not one that benefits the insurance agent or the insurance company. Policies that accumulate a cash value are not effective investments as what you earn is basically a percentage of the life insurance company's investments that are left over after expenses. These products are really not meant to be used as a retirement tool in any sense as the returns they produce are low in reality. If you are in need of insurance and do not trust yourself to save they are better than not saving at all and do provide some cash value. But as it was stated before if you are in need of 30 years of insurance buy a 30 year term policy and invest the difference in a more efficient investment such as a mutual fund or exchange traded fund that have low expenses and are efficient over long periods of time. Again do not buy something you do not need so examine your situation and do what is best for you and your loved ones.

Many insurance agents will suggest you purchase permanent life policies because they will get paid a higher commission as compared to a level term policy. Also insurance companies do not necessarily like it when someone decides that they will cancel a permanent policy and take their cash value. In many instances they will try to persuade the insured to take a loan out against the policy to pay the premiums and keep the policy in force. And not only were you not able to do what you wanted you are now paying the insurance company interest on borrowing your own money. This is why term insurance may be the better choice for many as it is just insurance plain and simple. Many people will buy a term policy to provide coverage for their loved ones when they are younger, are still working, and have obligations to meet regardless. In many instances the insurance is not needed when the term expires as the insurer is now in theory self-insured. Most people do not need insurance in their retirement years as their children are grown, the mortgage is paid off, and as they are retired there is no need to replace any income. And in the event that insurance is still needed most insurance companies will allow the insured to renew the policy with higher premiums to reflect their advanced age with no additional underwriting. Or if the policy is convertible the insured has the option of having the term policy become a permanent policy with higher premiums to reflect your current age and new type of policy.

Now that you have taken all of this into account it is time to figure out how much coverage you do in fact need. First you need to ask yourself how much debt you have that will have to be paid off in the event of your death. Add all of your debts up and that is the minimum amount of coverage you will need as you do not want your loved ones to be left to pay off your debts after you have died and your earning income is no longer available. Now income replacement is where you will get into some large figures as you decide how much of your income will need to be replaced. In theory you will want to have a policy that is large enough that your loved ones can live off of the interest the death benefit provides. As an example, you had a $500,000 policy and it earns a 9% return that means it will replace $45,000 a year towards your lost income without using any of the original $500,000 death benefit. But in the event the interest earned is only 8% the lost income will only be paid at $40,000 meaning the additional $5,000 that was not earned has to be done without by your loved ones or they take it out of their principal and reduce the $500,000 by $5,000. Another thing that needs to be factored into your calculation is any future obligation that you may want to fund such as a child's college education. One aspect that really does not come into the equations is the insurance cost on someone who does not contribute to the overall financial stability of the family. While the loss of a child would be devastating to a parent or parents their death only creates minor final expenses that most families can absorb and if they are not in a position to pay for a funeral it may be acceptable to maintain a small life insurance policy on the child but under no circumstance should the policy be more than what the expected final expenses will be. After you have added up all of these factors that will give you a good starting point for how much insurance you will need. Also most insurance companies have on-line life insurance calculators that you can use to estimate your need. If you have a very complex need or situation it may be best to consult a financial planner or insurance advisor to ensure you have a product that matches you need at a level sufficient to meet all of your loved one's needs.

Riders to Consider

Now you have your life insurance policy after deciding on what type of insurance you need to protect your family, how long will need the insurance, and for how much coverage you will be needing. However, insurance companies offer additional specialized coverage or terms in conjunction with your policy called riders. These are basically add-ons that will provide additional peace of mind concerning your policy and they come at a price depending on what benefits the rider provides. Now riders will vary from insurance company to insurance company and many provide some of the more basic riders at low costs or even free to the policy owner.

One of the riders that costs the insured an extra premium is the waiver of premium rider. This rider will step in after an elimination period and suspend the cost of the premium in the event the insured becomes totally disabled and cannot work.

With this rider the insured will not have to decide between the basics of living and funding their life insurance policy when they cannot work. This rider will generally expire when the insured reaches the age of 65.

A related rider which is more expensive is the disability income rider. This rider will provide an income to the insured in the event they meet the definition of disabled as defined by the insurance company. Now each insurance company has a different definition of disabled so be sure to read and thoroughly understand your company's definition. Now this rider will not replace 100% of your income and most insurance companies have at least two part formula option to determine the rider's benefit to the insured. That is the insurance company will replace up to 60% of the insured's income provided that amount does not exceed 1.5% or 2% of the face value of the death benefit. It is important to know if the rider will pay for an injury resulting only from an accident or if it include illnesses that prevent the insured from working. Also these riders will only provide the income benefit for a specified period of time usually for a maximum of two years. Another aspect of this rider that is important to know and understand is if you are covered if you cannot work in your own occupation or in any occupation. The cost of this rider is dependent on what injuries are covered, the percentage of the insured's salary is paid as a benefit, and if it cover the insured's own occupation or any occupation. And a final thought on the disability income rider is some insurance companies will not coordinate with any other types of insurance while others will pay the benefit regardless if the insured has other forms of disability coverage.

The guaranteed insurability rider is one that may or may not be provided for free by insurance companies. This rider will allow the insured to purchase additional coverage at a later date without having to provide any additional medical information to the insurance company. Regardless of the insured's insurability they are guaranteed coverage provided they exercise the rider prior to their policy expiring. As a rule this rider will allow the insured to buy additional coverage at predetermined intervals or ages that are established in the rider itself. While this rider will guarantee the insurability it does not guarantee what the premiums will be as those will be determined at the age of the insured when the additional coverage is purchased.

Now many younger individuals and families buy term coverage due to the fact that they are just starting out in the careers and cannot afford permanent insurance policies. The term conversion rider is a solution to this situation. This rider allows the insured to convert a term policy into a permanent policy that will provide a death benefit for the insured's life and not just the length of the term. When this rider is used the insured generally will convert their term policy to a permanent one without having to undergo a medical exam which basically takes a component of the guaranteed insurability rider. Most insurance companies will have a deadline in the term which the policy must be converted prior to meeting. In many of these riders the insured must convert the term policy prior to the last five years of the term's policy or age 65. It is very important that the insured understands the provisions of this rider as they may differ from insurance company to insurance company.

In today's world there is a high probability that someone could die as a result of an accident as compared to natural causes. The accidental death rider provided additional coverage for the insured in such events and normally doubles the death benefit, although some insurance companies will have a maximum death benefit that can be paid under this rider. It is relatively inexpensive and can even be bought as a standalone policy though it is normally cheaper if bought as a rider to an existing life insurance policy. Also many insurance companies will even provide this rider at no additional cost to the insured. Another feature of this rider is that in the event of a full or partial dismemberment such as the loss of a limb or the insured's eyesight a portion of the death benefit will be paid as compensation for this loss. The insured's occupation and hobbies will aid in determining the premiums for this rider as some occupations or hobbies are considered more dangerous than other and thereby more likely to result in accidental deaths.

Two riders that are similar in nature and can be used in conjunction with one another are the accelerated death benefit and critical illness rider. Many insurance companies do provide these riders at no cost to the insured provided they meet the policy's guidelines. Under the accelerated death benefit the insurance company will pay a percentage of the death benefit or a maximum amount to the insured in advance of their death provided they have a terminal illness and have less than a year to live. Some policies will extend the life expectancy to two years for terminal illnesses that have properly diagnosed. The proceeds of the policy can be used to pay for any expenses that the insured has and any amount that is paid as an accelerated portion will be deducted from the face amount of the death benefit upon the insured's death. The critical illness rider will pay the insured in the event they contract one of the covered illnesses as spelled out in the policy's rider. These are normally cancer, stroke, heart attack, or kidney failure. In many instances one or both of these riders will be applied if the insured is going to be confined to a long-term care facility and will need the proceeds of the life insurance policy to pay for the care. This is not to be confused to the long-term care rider that will be a rider that the insured pays for but in the event the insured is confined to a long-term care facility the insurance company will pay the costs as dictated by the terms of the long-term care rider.

The final rider that will be examined is the return of premium rider. This rider is for term life insurance policies and is fairly expensive as it guarantees that in the event that the insured lives to the end of the life insurance's term and has not utilized the benefits the insurance company will refund all or a portion of the premiums paid for the life insurance policy. As a general rule insurance companies will offer a 50% return of premium or a 100% return of premium. Depending on which percentage of the premiums the insured wishes to be returned help in determining the price of the rider. The higher the amount that will be returned will result in a higher premium.

Should You Cash In Your Policy

People will have a wide range of reasons for canceling a policy or taking a loan out against the cash value of the policy. Most people at some point or another will experience some form of a financial hardship during their lifetime. In most instances these financial difficulties are temporary and can be overcome. But in some instances the financial hardship may be prolonged and turning to the cash value of your permanent life insurance policy is certainly an option. But just because it is an option does not mean you should turn to it for the cash you need at that point in time. If by accessing your policy's cash value you could possibly harm your family's financial future in the event you die it may not be worth the risk. But as in life nothing is certain and it may be necessary for the insured to access the cash value if no other options are available.

Permanent life insurance builds a cash value of reserves through excess premiums that the insurer paid plus any accrued interest that has been earned. These funds are always kept segregated from the life insurance death benefits reserves due to a legal responsibility of the insurance company. If in the event you do need to access your cash value of your policy you can do this through a loan or a full or partial surrender of the policy. Another option that is available in some states is where the insured sells their policy for cash through a method called life settlement where you are paid a percentage of the death benefit and the person or company that bought the policy will ensure the premiums are paid and they will collect the death benefit upon the insured's death.

There are some benefits to a withdrawal over a loan when it comes to the cash value of the policy. Generally a life insurance company will allow limited withdrawals of cash depending on the type of policy that is owned and the issuing company. One main advantage of a withdrawal over a loan is that they are not taxable up to the policy's basis and the loan and interest do not have to be repaid. That is provided that the policy is not classified as a modified endowment contract. But before a withdrawal is made the insured needs to consider that a reduced cash value could also cause a reduction in the face of the death benefit. A reduction of the death benefit could have negative consequences on the insured's loved ones as that could be money that was intended to replace the insured's income. A withdrawal is not always tax free depending on how old the policy is as policies under 15 years in length are generally subject to tax. And a withdrawal is always taxable to the extent that it exceeds the insured's cost basis. Any event that reduces the cash value could cause the premiums to increase in order to maintain the face death benefit. Now if the policy is considered a modified endowment contract any withdrawal prior to age 59 ½ will be assessed a 10% early withdrawal penalty as well as income tax as the policy is treated as an annuity and thereby considered a retirement account.

As far as loans are concerned the insurance company will loan the insured some amount using the cash value of the policy as collateral. Depending on the policy and issuing company some loans will be at a fixed interest rate while others could be variable interest rates. Also, considering that most people who take out loans on their life insurance policies may be experiencing financial hardships there is no need to qualify for a loan from your own life insurance policy. The amount you can borrow is dependent on the value of the cash in the account and the terms of the policy. Now you are also under no obligation to repay the loans although interest will be accruing and any unpaid balance at the time of the insured's death could reduce the face amount of the death benefit.

In the event you surrender and cancel the policy the insurance company will issue the insured a check for the full amount contained in the cash value. If the policy is canceled early in the life of the policy surrender charges may apply thereby reducing the amount that will be issued to the insured. While the insurance is no longer in effect the insured is free to use the accumulated cash value they receive in any manner they see fit. But anyone who surrenders their policy needs to be aware that taxes may be owed on a portion of the amount received when it is in excess of the cost basis paid by the insured. As you are in fact canceling your life insurance policy it is best to ensure that the policy and by extension the death benefits are no longer needed for loved ones.

The final option to cashing out one's life insurance policy is when you sell it as a life settlement. In theory someone who is need of money will sell their policy to an individual or a life-settlement company for a percentage of the cash death benefit that will be paid upon the insured's death. The new owner will pay the premiums and keep the policy in place in order to collect the full death benefit. But there are certain restrictions that must be met prior to selling your policy as a life-settlement. The insured must be at least 65 years old, have a life expediency of 15 years or less, and a death benefit of at least $100,000. A life-settlement is normally done when the percentage that the insured gets of the death benefit by selling the policy is greater than the accumulated cash value. And as a general rule the money received from a life-settlement that in excess of the cost basis is taxed as ordinary income. While a life-settlement does provide liquidity the insured needs to consider that they are giving up control of their life insurance policy, the buyer of the policy will have access to the insured's medical records and could request medical updates, there is little or no regulation of the life-settlement industry, and they have extremely high commissions which reduce the amount of money the insured will receive.

About the Author

Kirk G. Meyer's educational and work background is fairly diverse. He holds a BS in Business Administration from Haskell Indian Nations University in Lawrence, Kansas and a MBA and MS in Accounting from Strayer University in Washington, DC. He also just received a MS in Financial Planning from Bentley University in suburban Boston, Massachusetts. Mr. Meyer works for the federal government in the area of contracts and prior to his current position was a bank examiner for a federal regulatory agency. In addition to his education and work experience, he is also a registered independent life insurance agent in his home state of Tennessee selling various life insurance products and annuities to individuals and families in need of these types of products. His educational background and love of helping others make him an asset to those looking for assistance and guidance in financial and personal financial matters.